Hip Hind Hook
Nigel Pantling

smith|doorstop

Published 2018 by Smith|Doorstop Books
The Poetry Business
Campo House,
54 Campo Lane,
Sheffield S1 2EG
www.poetrybusiness.co.uk

ISBN 978-1-912196-16-6
Designed & Typeset by Utter
Printed by Biddles

Smith|Doorstop books are a member of Inpress:
www.inpressbooks.co.uk. Distributed by NBN International, Airport
Business Centre, 10 Thornbury Road Plymouth PL 6 7PP.

The Poetry Business gratefully acknowledges the support of
Arts Council England.

Supported by
ARTS COUNCIL
ENGLAND

Contents

In Memory of Colonel Jasper Browell MBE 1928–2017

'The Officer who does not learn from his mistakes in peacetime is undertaking to repeat them in war.'

– The Regimental Officer's Tactical Manual for Warfare in Europe Section 0.1.3

Marching In with the Regimental Quarter Master Sergeant

I always like to be here myself, Sir,
when a young officer takes over his first married quarter.
I wouldn't want one of my clerks to march you in
and forget to tell you to count the cutlery
or say you're only entitled to two Chairs Easy Officers:
I'll get another one sent over from the stores tomorrow.

Look closely at the glasses, Sir, and refuse the chipped ones,
or you'll have to pay for them when you March Out.
By the way, Sir, it's the same furniture next door, and in every Type B Quarter,
so you and your good lady wife will feel at home when you visit the neighbours.
I'm sorry about the carpet, Sir, I know it only covers three quarters of the floor.
You have to be a major before it reaches the walls.

On the Young Officers' Course

'Understanding your enemy's capabilities
is the essential first step of defence'
– The Regimental Officer's Tactical Manual
for Warfare in Europe, Section 5.7.21

Lieutenant Colonel Hough bridled at the strength of the Warsaw Pact.
At the 3rd Shock Army's three tank divisions with a thousand T54's,
at their heavy guns, twice as many as our artillery could muster,
at their massed motorised infantry in armoured personnel carriers
held in constant readiness to bull-doze through the British sector.
And had he mentioned the Scud missiles with nuclear warheads?

He prepared us well for war, even if the closest we came to seeing
a T54 or a Scud was propaganda footage of the May Day Parades,
armour and missiles rolling endlessly past the saluting Soviet,
in what (we now know) was a closed loop round a Moscow block.

Old Soldier's Warning

'A defending force must make the most of
the natural features of the ground which it holds'
  – The Regimental Officer's Tactical Manual
  for Warfare in Europe, Section 4.1.4

The Staff will say you have the upper hand
from fighting on familiar ground,
that Russian tanks can't breach the Ruhr woods,
their infantry won't wade across the Weser.

OK. You'll know the ranges from your annual camps,
their hills and tracks will soon become old friends.
But you won't fight the war on the ranges,
so how's that help when you're trying to deploy your guns

in a Hesse pig farm picked at random from the map?
The woods are dense it's true, but then the Ardennes were,
thirty years ago. And I've sailed the Weser: I could tack
from bank to bank in seconds. It won't hold them back.

Gunner R.

A Liverpool boy with a thick-cut accent,
he's the Battery Commander's driver:
always curious, always a camera to hand.
He speaks the language, which is unusual
and useful when the BC wants a bratwurst.
Also unusual: he has a girlfriend in Celle,
and an old Mercedes he drives to see her.
One night, on the road back from Celle,
he drives the Mercedes into an oak tree.
The engine ends up in his lap.
The Bundespolizei, in their curious custom,
send us their scene of crime photographs.

Second Lieutenant N.

Too clever for his own good is the general opinion:
a graduate among officers who all went straight
from school to Sandhurst. He tries to wear that lightly,
keeps the Mozart turned down, has the New Scientist
sent from England in a plain wrapper. And he's a prig:
shunning the lunchtime port, not joining in the games
or the elevation of dogs to honorary Mess membership.
What saves him is being good with his soldiers
and tactically stronger than his contemporaries.
His Confidential Report says 'in action, some officers think,
then run. Others run, then think. This officer
thinks as he runs'. He assumes this is a compliment.

Language Training

Captain Gwynfor Evans,
Royal Army Education Corps,
is teaching Colloquial German.

Ich bin ein britischer Soldat

Twenty of us sit at school desks,
with no allowance made for rank,
Regiment or length of leg,

Ich wohne und arbeite in Dortmund

learning the language as determined
by Gwynfor, who's sure he knows
exactly what soldiers need to get by.

Ich hätte gern noch ein Bier bitte

After two weeks we are sent into town
to test our skills on locals too polite
to reply using their perfect English.

Wie viel ist das Hündchen im Schaufenster?

Years later someone asks me
where I learnt to speak German
with such a sing-song accent.

Witness Statement

There was no panic.
All ranks were standing calmly well back from the gun platforms.
I could smell cordite, and observed smoke around the damaged gun.

I located the senior officer present, and asked about casualties.
None of the gun detachment had been struck by metal debris.
I found this most surprising.

However, several had burns to exposed skin, all were deafened,
some were blinded, and the No 1 was in such shock
he would not let go of the firing lanyard. I cut it from his grasp.

A close inspection confirmed the detonation of a shell within the breech.
The barrel had burst and peeled back like a banana:
several feet of rifled steel had vaporised.

The firing mechanism, projected back thirty feet,
had embedded in a tree trunk, taking with it on the way
the epaulette of the section commander.

That completes my report, Sir, except to say that in thirty years' service
I have seen nothing like this before.
I believe it will take much technical investigation to uncover the cause.

Might I suggest that the Americans may be able to help.
My driver tells me that they lost several guns this way in Vietnam,
before they sold these on to us.

Postcard from the Border 1

At sparrow-fart today, Jez, we set out in two land-rovers, just like yours on the farm only with locked boxes for the ammo, so we don't start a world war or shoot each other like you did me with your fucking air-gun in the hay barn. We jolted along this dirt track up the mountain, and all you could see was fir trees, and this sodding great peak on the other side of the border with radio aerials sprouting round the top.

Dinner in the Mess

Regimental silver down the centre of the table:
miniature six-pounders, Boer War howitzers,
five point fives from the Borneo campaign,
and, one-twentieth scale, the self-propelled M107
parked ready for war on the Regimental square.

Among the silver, branched candelabra – candles half-burnt
with red stalactites reaching the polished mahogany –
crested china under monogrammed linen napkins,
decanters scattering the candlelight in garnet and quartz
and glasses of port standing ready like ruby sentries.

Heads turn to the subaltern newly arrived from England,
the proud bearer of bad news. News of three-day weeks,
union unrest, striking miners, homes heated by paraffin
and lit by torches, firemen refusing to work, IRA bombs,
City banks going bust and savers losing everything.

He says the papers claim Heath's government's collapsing,
that Harold Wilson's a Communist, in hock to the unions.
Then the talk round the table is how soon the politicians
will fall back on the Army to be pit-workers, fire-fighters,
jacks of all civilian trades. Some ask, under their breath,

what if the consequence is chaos? Are the rumours true
of Generals ready to step in for the good of the country?
Through the clamour, the Mess President's gavel.
The new subaltern stands, port glass in hand,
'Gentlemen: the Queen, our Captain General'.

Tactical Exercise Without Troops

*'Instructors Of Gunnery must ensure Young Officers are rigorously trained ...
to keep their skills sharp'*
  – The Regimental Officer's Tactical Manual
    for Warfare in Europe, Section 2.7.3

The Instructors of Gunnery have brought us to a Hohne hilltop,
to practice target acquisition and coordination of artillery fire.

We have no supporting guns today: the IGs tell us
we have to pretend we see where the shells are landing.

Sounds simple, but my IG is good at changing things around.
When I tell him I've spotted an enemy patrol (invisible, of course)
and give him the bearing to that position,

he says forget it, *bring fire down*
on whale-backed wood, three quarters right, target: the launcher for a Scud.

I see no wood.
But understanding the urgency I choose a likely spot
and reel off firing orders as if I did,

then wait and watch
for make-believe shells from guns that aren't there to hit an imaginary scud

until my IG swears, and turning asks what grid I gave the guns.
You bloody fool. Your shells are landing on our own troops.

Mixed Doubles

I saw it happen. They'd been playing tennis
on the court beside the Mess one Sunday morning:
a mixed doubles tournament, husbands and wives,
except that her husband preferred model railways
so she'd asked Jonny to stand in, and they'd won.

Afterwards they sat with the rest of us on the lawn.
We subalterns were doing our best to be pleasant
to the marrieds until the curry lunch was ready.
The Mess staff were pouring gin and tonic,
double strength, out of the crystal glass jugs.

He was wearing his watch on the arm nearest to her,
and as she leaned forward to read the time
she tucked her falling hair behind her ear,
took his hand, and lightly, so lightly,
ran her fingers along the inside of his wrist.

Bombardier B.

He could have been a magician in another life,
making things appear before your very eyes:
when the Bar was down by six beer barrels
before a stock-take, he helped the NAAFI staff
lift the four remaining barrels on their lorry.
Later they swore on oath they'd loaded ten.
He can also make himself invisible:
he once played the enemy on a divisional exercise
and a patrol of Green Jackets, keyed for ambush,
stepped unknowing over his camouflaged body.
Sadly, he can make things disappear, too,
which gets in the way of further promotion.

Captain A.

He lives beyond his means to run an old Morgan,
and his unpaid Mess bills are large enough
to be contrary to good order and military discipline.
He avoids court martial for debt, but only because
the Colonel admires his car and turns a blind eye.
Obsessed with Arabia, he has erected in his room
a marquee borrowed from the regimental stores
in which he sits wearing a fez, smoking a hookah.
Soldiering comes easy to him, and his eccentricity
and good humour endear him to all ranks. Later,
he'll transfer to the Trucial Oman Scouts, to serve
with quiet distinction and rather lower Mess bills.

Early Morning Call

'Regular unannounced practice of wartime deployment is essential'
– The Regimental Officer's Tactical Manual
for Warfare in Europe, Section 3.4.49

That August night, at precisely o three hundred hours,
the red telephone rang in the orderly officer's room.
My good friend Ashman, who the day before
had scored the century that won us the Garrison Cup,
stirred, picked up the receiver, listened and repeated back
the top secret Codeword. The Codeword which when
checked in the Black Book in the safe beside his bed
required the immediate mobilisation of our Regiment
from its Fallingbostel barracks to a secure forest hide
as specified in the Corps Commander's plan for war.

How we'd practised for that telephone call:
the C.O. alerted first, then messages cascading
from majors to captains to subalterns;
the duty sergeant rousing the sergeants' mess
alarms sounding in the barrack blocks
the guard turning out to open stores and shutters
and warm up the engines on the tracked vehicles;
so within thirty minutes of receiving the Codeword
the Commanding Officer could give his orders
and the Battery Commanders lead the guns
rattling out the garrison gates as if it was for real.

Except that at three o one on that August morning
Lieutenant Ashman, replacing the receiver in its cradle,
also replaced his head on the pillow. At o eight thirty,
as he and I reminisced about his batting over our usual
Eggs Benedict, toast and coffee in the Officers Mess,
the Corps Commander was approaching the empty hide.

Hip Hind Hook

'All ranks must be trained to identify Warsaw Pact weaponry
and to refer to it by the approved NATO code names'
– The Regimental Officer's Tactical Manual
for Warfare in Europe, Section 7.5.23

Yesterday it was helicopters.
Hip, the one which has rockets.
Hind, with multi barrelled machine guns.
Hook, carrying troops. Or was it
the other way round?
Now we're on to anti-tank missiles.
They must be easier to remember ...
Snapper, Swatter, Sagger, Spigot.

Postcard from the Border 2

When you get to the border, guess what?
There's nothing there: just some crappy
wooden post stuck in the ground, two foot
high and striped red, yellow and black.
Turns out, Jez, the actual fence is a
hundred yards back. Mind, you can still
see it's razor wire, so much the worse for
any poor bastard that tries to climb it, and
that's assuming he can get past the car
traps, the fucking scary dogs, the minefield.

Detente

In Moscow, Nixon and Brezhnev
are warming to each other
and moving towards SALT.

In East Berlin, Willy Brandt
is meeting Willi Stoph
to promote his Ostpolitik.

In Fallingbostel, I'm off duty
and in my room with Hildegard
whose English is good enough
to encourage our Entspannung.

O Group

Orders, Gentlemen, received from Divisional HQ at zero four thirty hours today.

Situation.

We are in support of Blue Force: Blue Force's forward battalions are located in defensive positions here and here with concentrations of armour and anti-tank weapons here, here and here.

Red Force is reported as advancing rapidly westward in greatly superior strength with columns of armour supported by mechanised infantry, medium and heavy artillery and battlefield nuclear weapons.

Mission.

Blue Force's mission is to deny Red Force access to the central European plain by holding the ground west of this line here and channelling the enemy into killing grounds here and here where he can be destroyed by armour and artillery.

This regiment's mission is to support Blue Force by deploying to gun positions here, here and here from which to engage targets in the killing grounds as identified by our forward observation posts on these ridge lines here and here.

Execution.

Blue Force intelligence has reported that from zero seven hundred hours the enemy will seek to disrupt our defensive positions by the use of nuclear missiles and artillery with biological and chemical warheads.

We expect that the fall-out from these weapons will spread from here to here and that the regiment's observation posts, gun positions, forward and rear echelons and the routes between them will all be affected.

At zero six thirty hours all ranks will adopt full protective measures, wearing NBC suits, gloves, overshoes and gas masks at all times, closing and pressurising armoured vehicles and remaining inside them whenever possible.

I do not need to remind you, Gentlemen, of the consequences of failure to observe these orders.

Sergeant H.

Cabbage Head they call him,
weak at reading, weaker still at writing.
But as a Gun Number One,
it's once learned, never forgotten.
Technically he's the strongest,
his gun-crew the best trained. Each year
they win the inter-Regimental Best Gun Cup,
firing two rounds twenty seconds apart
to hit the same target simultaneously.
This piece of magic earns him status:
at dinner in the Sergeants Mess, the RSM
proposes the toast 'To Cabbage Head'.

Major K.

When in barracks, he spends his day on horseback.
Stick and ball at the Hussars' ground in the morning,
hacking with his dog across the Heide in the afternoon.
Recently, he's shown an affection for lunchtime port,
and his horse has been coming back on its own.
Everyone assumes he's disappointed he did badly
as a Battery Commander (sergeants don't trust him;
subalterns ignore him). He doesn't talk about it.
Nor does he talk about still being single at forty-two:
that's something no-one else dare raise. They could
mention the drinking, but they won't, and he will be
dead from liver failure well before retirement age.

The Adjutant's Desk

Front left, the signed Part Two orders for tomorrow's routine,
cyclostyled and ready to be issued at precisely 1600 hours.
Front right, the list of Orderly Officer duties for the next month:
Lieutenant Ashman has fourteen in a row for being idle.
Back right, the discharge instructions for Gunner Jones 362,
caught once too often with his hand in someone's pocket.
Back left, the court martial documents for Sergeant Davis,
four weeks Absent Without Leave when his wife left him.
In the centre, precisely framed by the spotless pad of
pink blotting paper, is the operational warning order
for another Northern Ireland tour, received in code
from MoD today, decrypted and annotated in black ink
Colonel, we shall be there over Christmas yet again:
expect discontent among the men with families.

Over Her Head

Wife of Major Clifton, allergic to her penicillin,
is waiting for the Registrar.

Next bed down, Wife of Captain Dalrymple
heavy with milk for her new daughter,

calls encouragement across the aisle
to Wife of Sergeant Edwards twelve days overdue.

Wife of Gunner Fincham, in the bed closest
to the clatter of the corridor, sleeps off her D and C.

Colonel Ronald Guthrie, Royal Army Medical Corps,
is late on his rounds but punctilious in his manner.

He will start with the senior wife present.

18 (Quebec 1759) Battery Waits for Orders

In the tense command post
the radio is an empty hiss.
Outside in the twilight
the guns crouch ready
under their camouflage,
crews keyed for action.
The Battery Sergeant Major
criss-crosses the gun position
checking sentries are alert.
In the air, a General's orders

You are to embark on the flat-bottomed boats
at midnight and drift in silence with the current.
Once at the beachhead, you will port your guns
up the Heights of Abraham, and engage the enemy.
Remember what your country expects from you
and be resolute in the execution of your duty.

Postcard from the Border 3

We can see these wooden watchtowers full of border guards pointing their sniper rifles and machine guns. So we get out of the vehicles with our own weapons – unloaded, but they don't know that do they – and our officer lines us up along the border like a row of cardboard practice targets while he counts the guards in the towers. I ask you Jez what the flying fuck is that all about?

Night Deployment

'Artillery ... must be fully capable of fire and movement by night as well as by day'
– The Regimental Officer's Tactical Manual for Warfare in Europe, Section 7.7.21

Dusk: the skylarks are settling to earth. Hedges and fields distill to a blur
as his recce party stops, hushed, lights off at the edge of a wood.

He treads the tree line, picking out platforms for the guns to lodge on,
unreeling the white tape that marks their way in,

then finds roosts for the Command Posts deep in the pines,
and deeper still for ammo wagons, cooks and water carriers.

Midnight: his white web complete, key points lit by pin bulbs like glow worms,
sentries out to meet and guide the guns,

and there's time for a brew and an egg banjo, to catnap under the scrim,
to read poetry by shaded torchlight or write letters home.

When the guns are in, and before the first recoil can spoil the night,
he'll be off to recce some other wood, in time for dawn.

Stammlager 311c

You might think it was why we didn't mix with the locals:
that we wouldn't share public transport with people

who could have seen the cattle trucks of Russians and Poles,
and the sick Jews from other camps brought there to die;

or we didn't want to eat in the Hof Der Heidmark
in case we were served by women who'd heard of the starvation

and smelt the typhus across the ten miles as the wind blows;
or it wasn't possible to buy bread at the Vatter Bakerai

because old Herr Vatter might have been ordered to help bury
the thirteen thousand who were liberated but didn't survive.

The truth is that few of us knew much about Bergen-Belsen:
perhaps that Anne Frank had died there, or that Pierrepoint

had hanged the Commandant. Even fewer visited to observe
the burned huts, the mass graves, the guilty silence of the birds.

Sergeant Major C.

Twelve years' service is fast to sergeant major.
Impeccably turned out, quick on the uptake,
reliable to the point of being predictable,
consistent with soldiers, he takes no nonsense.
Skilled too in handling his seniors: his quiet
'I wouldn't do that if I were you, Sir'
has saved several subalterns' careers.
His self-assurance and gift of the gab
will carry him on to be RSM
and then, if he wants it, to a commission.
In the Officers Mess, he'll be smart enough
not to forget where he comes from.

Colonel Jasper

Appointed to turn round a failing Heavy Regiment,
he has stamped his personality on it with a fierceness
consistent with his ginger hair and bristling moustache.
He's old world: values manners, a sense of tradition
and commitment in officers; loyalty and common sense
in other ranks. Those who don't match up soon know it.
His single-minded pursuit of the Regiment's interests
has earned him few friends at Divisional Headquarters.
He's served before in the Kings Troop, so his officers
are expected to play polo on Sundays, and to bring
their wives to tread-in between chukkas. He's pleased
that outsiders call the Regiment 'Jasper's Heavy Horse'.

Spurs

He weighs the spur in his open hand,
the fluted rowel sharp on his palm.
Running his thumb along the shank
and curved yoke, he homes the spigot
neatly in the heel of the black leather boot.

He was never asked to wear them in anger.
For his generation spurs were decorative,
only to be seen on ceremonial occasions.
But ah, then, their jingle as he marched,
their glitter as they split the sunlight.

Now, after disappointed years at a Staff desk,
he's springing the spurs from their heel-boxes,
wrapping them in tissue, to be stored safely
deep inside his boots. He doesn't see the paper
is smeared red, where a rowel has cut him.

Crossing Over

'Visible armed presence at the Inner German Border
is an essential element of deterrence'

   – The Regimental Officer's Tactical Manual
   for Warfare in Europe, Section 1.7.14

Sometimes, in that strange proximity to the Border
where each side is watching the other
and reading into every gesture
an understanding of lives
away from the fence,
a mood takes us

and at a signal
as if we're on parade
we rest our rifles on the ground
wave to our counterparts in the towers
and hop, step and jump twenty yards into the GDR,
where we pose for photographs to send to our families.

Author's note

With the exception of Colonel Jasper Browell, the characters in this book are works of my imagination and any resemblance to actual persons, living or dead, is purely coincidental.

The Regimental Officer's Tactical Manual for Warfare in Europe does not exist.